DK READERS is a compelling program for beginning readers, designed in conjunction with leading literacy experts, including Dr. Linda Gambrell, Distinguished Professor of Education at Clemson University. Dr. Gambrell has served as President of the National Reading Conference, the College Reading Association, and the International Reading Association.

Beautiful illustrations and superb full-color photographs combine with engaging, easy-to-read stories to offer a fresh approach to each subject in the series. Each DK READER is guaranteed to capture a child's interest while developing his or her reading skills, general knowledge, and love of reading.

The five levels of DK READERS are aimed at different reading abilities, enabling you to choose the books that are exactly right for your child:

Pre-level 1: Learning to read
Level 1: Beginning to read
Level 2: Beginning to read alon
Level 3: Reading alone
Level 4: Proficient readers

D1248641

The "normal" age at which a child begins to read can be anywhere from three to eight years old. Adult participation through the lower levels is very helpful for providing encouragement, discussing storylines, and sounding out unfamiliar words.

No matter which level you select, you can be sure that you are helping your child learn to read, then read to learn!

LONDON, NEW YORK, MUNICH,
MELBOURNE, AND DELHI

Series Editor Deborah Lock
U.S. Editor Shannon Beatty
Designer Vikas Sachdeva
Project Designer Akanksha Gupta
Art Director Martin Wilson
Production Editor Sarah Isle
Jacket Designer Natalie Godwin

Reading Consultant
Linda B. Gambrell, Ph.D.

First American Edition, 2012
12 13 14 15 16 10 9 8 7 6 5 4 3 2 1
001-184582-June 2012
Published in the United States by DK Publishing
375 Hudson Street, New York, New York 10014

DK books are available at special discounts when purchased in bulk for sales
promotions, premiums, fund-raising, or educational use.
For details, contact:
DK Publishing Special Markets
375 Hudson Street
New York, New York 10014
SpecialSales@dk.com

A catalog record for this book is available from the Library of Congress.

ISBN:978-0-7566-9276-6 (Paperback)
ISBN: 978-0-7566-9277-3 (Hardcover)

Color reproduction by Colourscan, Singapore
Printed and bound in China by L.Rex Printing Co., Ltd.

The publisher would like to thank the following for their kind permission to
reproduce their photographs:
(Key: a-above; b-below/bottom; c-center; f-far; l-left; r-right; t-top)

3 **Getty Images:** Asia Images. 4 **Corbis:** Peter Burian (c); Thomas Marent /
Visuals Unlimited (tl). **Getty Images:** Art Wolfe / Stone (b). 5 **Corbis:** DLILLC
(tr); Visuals Unlimited (c). 6-7 **Getty Images:** Asia Images. 6 **Photolibrary:**
Jurgen & Christine Sohns / FLPA (br). 7 **Corbis:** Thomas Marent, / Visuals
Unlimited (t). **Getty Images:** Daniel Berehulak / Staff / Getty Images News
(br). **Photolibrary:** Stockbrokerxtra Images (bc). 8 **Corbis:** Thomas Marent /
Visuals Unlimited (br). 9 **Corbis:** Thomas Marent / Visuals Unlimited (br).
Getty Images: Luciano Candisani / Minden Pictures (c). **Photolibrary:** Terry
Whittaker / FLPA (bc). 10 **Dreamstime.com:** Lasse Kristensen (c). **Getty
Images:** Creative Crop / Digital Vision (cr); Ultra.F / Digital Vision (cb). 11
Getty Images: Rubberball / Erik Isakson. **Photolibrary:** Stockbrokerxtra Images
(bc). 12-13 **Photolibrary:** Juniors Bildarchiv. 13 **Getty Images:** Pete Mcbride /
National Geographic (b). **Photolibrary:** Juergen and Christine Sohns (crb). 14
Getty Images: Gerry Ellis / Minden Pictures (t). 15 **Corbis:** Herbert Kehrer (br).
Getty Images: Ingo Arndt / Minden Pictures. **Photolibrary:** Cyril Ruoso (bl).
16-17 **Getty Images:** Piotr Naskrecki / Minden Pictures. 16 **Getty Images:** SA
Team / Foto Natura / Minden Pictures (bl); Kevin Schafer / Minden Pictures
(br). 17 **Getty Images:** Stan Osolinski / Oxford Scientific (br). **Photolibrary:**
Juniors Bildarchiv (bl). 18 **Getty Images:** Reinhard Dirscherl / WaterFrame (bl).
18-19 **Photolibrary:** Luiz C Marigo. 19 **Getty Images:** Reinhard Dirscherl /
WaterFrame (bc); Claus Meyer / Minden Pictures (bl). 20 **Science Photo
Library:** Chris Hellier (clb). 20-21 **Alamy Images:** Chris Hellier. 21 **Getty
Images:** Christian Kober / Robert Harding World Imagery (bc); Thomas
Marent / Minden Pictures (br). **Photolibrary:** Nick Garbutt (bl). 22 **Getty
Images:** Keren Su / Photodisc (t); Tier Und Naturfotografie J & C Sohns / The
Image Bank (bl). 23 **Getty Images:** Ben Cranke / The Image Bank; Lori Epstein
/ National Geographic (br). 24 **Corbis:** Peter Burian (c). **Getty Images:** Brooke
Whatnall / National Geographic (bl). 25 **Corbis:** Anup Shah (bl). **Getty
Images:** Fuse (br); Copyright Tony Franco / Flickr. 26-27 **Getty Images:** Visuals
Unlimited, Inc. / John Abbott. 26 **Photolibrary:** Michel & Christine
Denis-Huot (t). 27 **Corbis:** DLILLC (br). **Getty Images:** Steve Allen /
Photodisc (bc); Ben Cranke / The Image Bank (bl). 28-29 **Getty Images:** Sune
Wendelboe / Lonely Planet Images. 28 **Corbis:** Martin Harvey (bl). 29 **Corbis:**
Darrell Gulin (bl). **Photolibrary:** Christian Heinrich (bc); Keith Levit (br). 30
Dreamstime.com: Robert Wisdom (bl). **Getty Images:** Fotosearch. 31 **Corbis:**
Herbert Kehrer (cb). **Photolibrary:** Berndt Fischer (t); National Geographic
Society (br). 32 **Corbis:** Tim Davis (cb); DLILLC (ca); Oliver Lassen (b).
Dreamstime.com: Michael Lynch (t).

Jacket images: Front: **naturepl.com:** Nick Garbutt

All other images © Dorling Kindersley
For further information see: www.dkimages.com

Discover more at
www.dk.com

Contents

DK READERS

LEARNING
pre-level
1
TO READ

Monkeys

DK Publishing

Smile, please!
Come and meet
the monkeys of
the world.

A pygmy marmoset can fit in your hand. It's the smallest monkey.

marmosets

claw

tail

Golden lion tamarins climb up tree trunks and run along branches.

tamarins

golden
fur

branch

Capuchin monkeys eat fruit and insects, and even crabs and eggs.

fruit

crab / \ insects

capuchins

A squirrel monkey jumps from tree to tree. Its baby hangs on.

squirrel monkeys

baby

hand

13

arm

A spider monkey uses its tail to hang from a tree.

spider monkeys

_ tail

Howler monkeys call to each other. They are the loudest land animals.

howlers

ear

mouth

fur

eye

night monkeys

Night monkeys have
large brown eyes
to see in the dark.

Proboscis monkeys
have a huge nose
and a big belly.

nose

proboscis monkeys

belly

snow

Japanese macaques
keep warm in
the hot springs.

 macaques

hot
spring

A large mandrill
shows its teeth
to make friends
or scare foes.

nose

teeth

feet

vervet monkeys

Vervet monkeys
help each other
to keep clean.

___fur

A troop of baboons travels and lives together.

baboons

Which monkey

The monkeys rest
after being so busy.
Shh!

id you like best?

Glossary

Claw
a sharp nail on the end of an animal's hands or toes

Fur
a thick coat of soft hair that covers an animal's skin

Tail
a long, movable body part joined to an animal's bottom

Teeth
these are used for biting and chewing food

Troop
a group of monkeys, also called a tribe